MAKING
MATH WORKSHOP
WORK

Alex O'Connor
middle school math man

Alex O'Connor
Middle School Math Man
www.middleschoolmathman.blogspot.com

TABLE OF CONTENTS

Introduction

"Things turn out best for people who make the best of the way things turn out."

-John Wooden

INTRODUCTION

Teaching middle school math is unlike any other profession. This is probably best depicted by the reaction I receive every time somebody asks me what I do for a living. If you teach middle school, I'm sure you have all been there before. The exchange goes something like this:

Person: "So, what do you do for a living?"

Me: "I teach middle school math. I have a couple classes of 6th grade math and an 8th grade math class."

Person: (eyes go wide) "Woah. I don't know how you do it. I could never do that."

Not that teaching other grades isn't challenging… it is. Teaching in general is, in my opinion, more challenging than almost any other profession. Teaching middle school math presents its own set of challenges. Trying to coordinate a group of 25+ eleven year old children, who are often more concerned about their social interactions than learning math, to write and solve a two-step equation is not an easy task. Not to mention the students that are coming from situations outside of school that most adults would find difficult to overcome.

This world of middle school math is where my teaching career has landed. After graduating from UW-Madison in 2009, I spent about one year as a substitute teacher in multiple school districts. It is funny how it works, that teachers fresh out of college often get thrown into the most difficult teaching position as a daily substitute! A quick 2-hour stint subbing in a kindergarten classroom made me realize that the upper grades was where I wanted to end up.

When a 6th grade math position opened up in a small, rural school district in Wisconsin, I jumped on the opportunity. For my first five years, I taught primarily 6th grade math. Since then, in addition to my 6th grade classes, I have added an 8th grade math class. Seeing the change in my students from 6th grade to 8th grade has been a valuable experience for me. It has allowed me to gain a better understanding of where my 6th grade students are headed and how I can help them in the classroom.

When I accepted my first job as a new teacher entering a middle school math classroom, I quickly realized how different my students were. My classes had a combination of students who had always excelled and enjoyed learning math, alongside students who had been continually frustrated and overwhelmed by math in their elementary years. My philosophy of teaching math formed and evolved from this quandary, in which virtually every teacher is faced. First, I wanted to challenge every student at the academic level they were at, so that they would be challenged but not frustrated. Of course, this is easier said than done, when you have students who still struggle to add 7 + 6 alongside students who can solve the equation $12x - 6 = 102$. Second, I wanted to make math fun. I quickly recognized that I had a group of students that were coming in with a negative attitude towards math. Many of the students in this group either were frustrated by the content, bored by the lesson/worktime structure of a typical math class, or some combination of the two. I knew if I could find a way to meet students at the level they were at, while also making the learning fun, I would be able to prevent some of these negative perceptions of math from occurring.

The structure of math workshop provided a perfect platform to keep students engaged, active, and learning math at their own level. In my opinion, there isn't one correct way to implement math workshop. Although there are some general routines and expectations that any classroom using a math workshop structure should have, it is important that you use your creativity to adapt math workshop to your classroom and your students. This book is not meant to be an exact guide for every teacher on how to set up workshop, but rather a framework and collection of ideas for you to pick and choose what works in your classroom. After all, you know your own students better than anyone! Whether you are just beginning to think about using math workshop or have already implemented math workshop in your classroom, I hope you can find bits and pieces of this book to incorporate into your daily routine.

1 THE MATH WORKSHOP STRUCTURE

When starting math workshop, it is important to first understand your current situation, limitations, and classes. The exact layout and structure of math workshop depends a lot on class length and class size. In my district, we have 90 minute blocks for math, with class sizes typically between 20-26 students. I consider this the ideal situation for math workshop: long class length and small class size. How you structure math workshop in your classroom might look different, depending on the size and length of your classes. In this chapter, I will give you a basic overview of how I have fit in math workshop to the ideal, 90 minute block class situation. It also includes some of the most important information about what happens at each center. For those of you with different class lengths or class sizes, don't worry, you won't be forgotten! In Chapter 2, we will look at how you can make math workshop work for you, given your situation.

With a full 90 minutes, I am able to incorporate a daily check assessment into every class period, before jumping into math workshop centers. As students walk in the door, they take a scratch piece of paper and begin working on what we call the "daily check." The daily check consists of four questions that assess the concept we learned on the previous day. The four questions increase in difficulty from beginning to an advanced level. I have a 6th grade and 8th grade set of exit slips that I use as my daily check problems each day. These daily checks are essentially a mini quiz to see if students understood and retained the lesson from the previous day. Once I have collected the daily check work from each student, we go over the four problems as a class. This serves as an effective review of the content from the last lesson. This entire daily check routine, from the moment students walk in, usually takes about 20 minutes of class time.

Typically, I will grade and enter 2-4 of these daily checks each week. I have found it helpful to grade most of them early in the year, while students are still getting into the routine. This ensures that they become accustomed to giving each daily check their best effort. As the year unfolds, I will usually scale back how many of these are entered into the gradebook.

After the daily check is complete, it is time for us to jump into the new mini-lesson for that day. If there is any math vocabulary needed for the lesson, students begin by writing these down in their notebooks. The mini-lesson for that day should be a brief overview of the new concept. When considering what type of problems to use in the mini-lesson, I usually ask myself, "What is the essential skill or concept I want students to learn for that day?" Or as Hoffer writes,

> Using the opening as a springboard, teachers then dive into a mini-lesson designed to orient students to

the purpose of the day's work, then introduce or revisit concepts and strategies that will be useful during independent work time. This whole-group instruction can be done in the form of a think-aloud demonstration or shared practice on a problem parallel to one that students will tackle later." (2012, p. 10)

It is important to realize that this does not need to be an extensive lesson, since you will be meeting with every student in a small group during math centers. When I first started math workshop, my lessons went too long because I felt like I needed to cover every single type of problem and that every student needed to fully understand the concept before moving into centers. In fact, they went so long that students began counting the number of times I dropped my dry-erase marker in front of the class. At the suggestion of one of my students, we began keeping a tally of these marker drops, which became quite humorous... and quite the competition between classes. Every class wanted to have the most Mr. O'Connor marker drops in their class! Remember, the mini-lesson doesn't have to be so long that you drop your marker six times in one class. It is perfectly fine if a group of your students leave this whole class lesson not quite grasping the concept. They will have 10-15 minutes of small group instruction to strengthen their understanding!

Each mini-lesson usually includes 2-3 problems that I do as a whole group and 2-3 problems that students try on their own. The length of these mini-lessons can vary depending on the concept, but mine typically take up 10-15 minutes of class. If it is a review concept, you may not spend much time on this lesson. If it is a new and difficult concept, you will probably want to use the full 15 minutes!

After the 20 minute daily check and the 10 minute lesson, that leaves about 60 minutes for math workshop centers and any sort of wrap-up you want to incorporate at the end of class. Students are divided into four groups, with each group consisting of 5-7 students. I consider 6 or less students per group to be ideal, 7 manageable, and anything over 7 ineffective. Therefore, if you have larger class sizes, be sure to read the next chapter on making math workshop work for different class lengths and class sizes. The four centers, detailed below, include the Teacher Center, Homework Center, Technology Center, and the Hands-On Center. When we break into the four groups after the mini-lesson, one group goes to each center to begin math workshop.

TEACHER CENTER

In my opinion, the teacher center of math workshop is the single biggest factor in making math workshop so effective. There are not many other class structures, if any, where you can meet with every student in a small group every day. In this small group, I can easily see exactly what level each student is at with the concept we are learning on that day. For students who are struggling with the concept, I can give instant feedback, which helps prevent that frustrated feeling that can be so demoralizing to students. For students who have easily grasped the new concept, I can provide more challenging problems.

The teacher center also holds students accountable for understanding the material. During my first year of teaching, I used a more traditional class structure, in which I taught a whole group lesson and students then had a class worktime to work on the homework for that day. I specifically remember students who "flew under the radar." They weren't particularly engaged in the lesson, didn't fully understand the material, but knew that I would probably be busy helping the students who asked questions during worktime. If they quietly worked on the homework, they could slide by without really grasping the concept.

When I began using math workshop, I found that students were more actively engaged in understanding the content during the mini-lesson because they knew they would have to come up to the front table and work with me in a small group setting. Now, there wasn't a way for them to slide by without getting extra help from me.

 To help meet every student at their level during the Teacher Center, I have created two sets of problems for every concept that we cover. These problems are printed, cut, and laminated on task cards the size of a half sheet of paper. The first set of task cards is a basic set of 2-4 problems for each concept that we learn. As students come up to the front table, they receive one of these task cards and begin working at their own pace.

During these initial few minutes of work, I am able to identify which students are struggling with the basic concept and which students have already grasped it. As I assist the students who are struggling, the other students work through the problems at their own pace. Once a student finishes the problems on the first task card, they are then able to move on to the second set of enrichment task cards. These problems cover the same concept, but require higher level thinking and arithmetic. It is incredible to watch students work through the challenge of these enrichment problems! When it is time to rotate centers, students stop working on their task card and move to the homework center.

The benefits of the Teacher Center are not limited to the additional academic support that you can give your students. Sometimes it is the students that give you the best ideas. During my first year of teaching, one of my 6th graders gave me the idea to turn the date on my daily schedule into a math problem, as pictured. I have used their idea ever since!

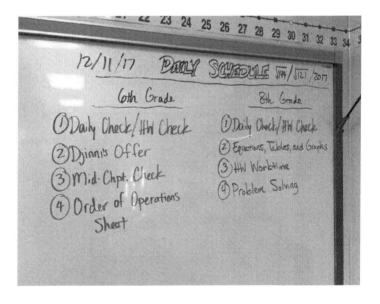

To make the Teacher Center simple and engaging for

students, I painted my front table using dry erase paint. I cannot tell you how much students love being able to use the white board table. It was a game changer when it comes to the engagement and effectiveness at my Teacher Center group! For more information on how I created the table and how it has held up, be sure to check out the White Board Table chapter later on in the book.

I rarely have students that finish the first task card and the enrichment task card during one fifteen minute rotation. However, if you do have a student that completes both sets of problems, there are a couple of options. If it is a student that you know would love a challenge, creating a bonus challenge on the fly at the front table is a fun option! I will sometimes create a really challenging computational problem in this scenario. For example, it is simple to create a difficult multiplying or dividing decimals problem on the spot.

I also have a weekly Challenge of the Week problem posted on my board. Students can enter this throughout the week on Monday through Thursday. Every Friday, we then go over the answer. Any students who were able to get the correct answer get a mint or Starburst! One of the greatest things about adding an 8th grade class, and an 8th grade Challenge of the Week problem, was when I started having 6th graders attempting to solve the 8th grade problems! The prize was upped to a pack of gum for any of these 6th graders that were able to answer the 8th grade challenge!

Another option for a student who finishes early at the front table is to have that student switch to the Homework Center a few minutes early. Chances are, there will only be a few minutes left until everyone rotates to their next center anyways. In this case, you could have the student begin working on homework a few minutes early. Finally, if the student can help another student at the Teacher Center, that is often the best option. Being able to explain the math to another student is a great skill. Additionally, students who need help are sometimes more likely to accept that help from one of their peers.

HOMEWORK CENTER

After completing the Teacher Center, students rotate directly to the Homework Center. This is each student's opportunity to individually practice the skills learned during the mini-lesson and the front table. I require students to work individually at their seat during this rotation. For my classes, the homework consists of about ten problems from the textbook series our district uses. Any problems that the students do not complete during their 10-15 minute Homework Center becomes homework for that night. I have found that most of my students are motivated to get their work done during this center. They are usually feeling pretty good about their understanding of the concept, since they have just left the Teacher Center, and they are driven by the fact that they want to finish their homework in class so they don't have to bring it home.

It is important to note that not every group will have the chance to meet with you at the Teacher Center before moving to the Homework Center. Since one group of students begins at each of the centers, you will have one group that starts their rotations at the Homework Center. It is important that this group includes students who you are confident will have a fairly solid understanding of the new concept after seeing the mini-lesson for that day. Therefore, this group typically includes my higher level students.

TECHNOLOGY CENTER

The final two centers, the Technology Center and Hands-On Center, are where you can really use your creativity as a teacher. These centers can be very fluid and often change depending on the day. For the Technology Center, I have used several different activities throughout the years. There is so much technology out there and you can base this center on the resources that you have available at your school. I originally used iPads as my primary tool during this center. My school has iPads available for checkout, loaded with math apps that students used during this time. I have gradually shifted to using my school's Chromebooks during this center. I have had success using both Khan Academy and IXL with my students. Both programs make it easy to set up a personal account for each student and track their progress as they work through problems.

To help with motivation during this center, I began conducting a Top Ten routine every Friday. Throughout the week, students work on their IXL or Khan Academy account. At the end of the day Thursday, these programs make it simple to track their progress for that week. I pick a category, such as problems answered correctly, and find which students were in the "Top Ten" for that category. The top student gets a pack of gum, second and third place get a piece of candy, and the students who were fourth through tenth place get a mint or Starburst. Nothing like a little extra edible motivation to get middle schoolers working!

HANDS-ON CENTER

The fourth center is the Hands-On Center. As I previously mentioned, this is another center that you can be creative with. This center is a great opportunity to make math fun and engaging for your students. I have personally spent hours finding and creating math games and activities for students to use during this center. One of my class favorites is the Area Invasion board game pictured below, in which students find the area of various polygons as they move around the game board. Finding games and activities similar

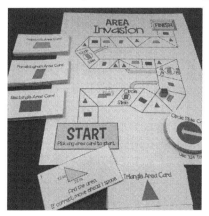

to this will make class more exciting than if you overload students with worksheets and practice problems. If you are interested in these activities, be sure to check out the Resources Index at the end of the book. It is essential that you find engaging activities for your students. As Hoffer states, "In order for students to devote their time in math class to reasoning and communicating as thoughtful mathematicians, we need to offer them something worthy to chew on with their intellectual teeth" (2012, p. 6).

Although this center can be a lot of planning and preparation, it is important to remember that it is perfectly okay to reuse math games and activities. Often times, I will use the same math game at this center for 2-3 consecutive days and then also bring back the game later in the year as a review. If you find the right activities that students enjoy, they won't mind playing it multiple times!

With that being said, if you are really feeling crunched on your prep time and can't get an activity ready, you can always have students use this time as a second Technology Center! Part of the beauty of the Hands-on Center is that it can really be whatever you want it to be.

2 Making Math Workshop Work

One of the most common questions that I have received when it comes to getting math workshop started is how to make it work given a specific class length and class size. "I have __ students and __ minute classes. How can I make math workshop work?" This chapter aims to give you practical ideas to help make math workshop work for you, given your specific situation. Because of the wide variety of class lengths and class sizes across districts and classrooms, math workshop isn't a one size fits all approach. You may need to choose one of these general outlines and adapt it to your students' needs.

As you read through these different setups, I encourage you to visualize how it would work with your specific classes. As you do this, there are two key factors to keep in mind. First, you should aim to keep each of your math workshop groups at six students or less. If you need to stretch a few groups to seven students that is okay, but anything higher than seven makes it very difficult to meet the needs of every student during their Teacher Center time. Second, the length of each of your rotations should be a minimum of about ten minutes. Anything less than that makes it difficult for students to be productive at each center.

Every Center Every Day
Works for: Long length and large class size OR medium length and small class size

If scheduling makes it possible, I feel like this is the ideal math workshop setting. If you have 60 minute classes, which I consider a medium length, and small class sizes this can work. This is the situation I had my first couple years of teaching. Students are divided into four groups, with four to six students in each group. In this situation, students travel to all four centers every day. I personally prefer a quick warm-up problem, a brief mini-lesson on the new concept, four 10 minute centers, and a brief wrap-up at the end of class. In this setting, timing is extremely important. Sixty minutes can go by fast and it is important you don't shortchange the last centers. It is also important to remember that the mini-lesson does not need to be an extensive lesson. It might be that you only have time for a few examples as a whole class before breaking into centers.

This also works with 80+ minute classes, which I consider a long length, and larger class sizes. With a larger class size, you could split students into five groups to keep each group size manageable. For example, a class of 30 split into 5 groups of 6 students. The five group option requires an extra center of planning, since students are in five groups and travel to 5 centers each day. I used this format for one year when we switched to 90 minute blocks and my class sizes were larger than normal. I divided my centers into a Teacher Center, Homework Center, Technology Center, Hands-on Center, and Problem Solving Center. During the additional Problem Solving Center, I used many of the free Problems of the Month, from the Inside Mathematics website. You can find out more about these in the Resources Index at the end of the book.

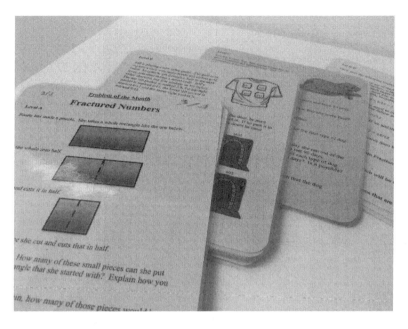

Lesson - Work Time - 2 Centers
Works for: Medium or long length and any class size

In this structure you would have a normal whole group warm-up and mini-lesson to introduce your new concept, which would last about 20-30 minutes. This would be followed by a 10-15 minute worktime for the whole class to start practicing on homework problems. After this short worktime, students would then be split into four groups. However, unlike the "Every Center Every Day" format above, each group only goes to two centers each day, each lasting about 10 minutes. For example, let's say we have students divided into groups A, B, C, and D. There are four different centers, but notice that none of the centers are a Homework Center. This is because the students will have already had a chance to work on homework as a class. This modified math workshop structure isn't ideal, but it still provides an opportunity for the teacher to meet in small groups with each student on most days. Since Group A and Group D end up meeting with the teacher three days per week, as opposed to two days per week like Group B and Group C, you may want to consider placing some of your struggling students in Group A and Group D.

	Monday	Tuesday	Wednesday	Thursday	Friday
Group A	1 – Teacher 2 – Prob. Solve	1 – Technology 2 – Teacher	1 – Hands-on 2 – Technology	1 – Prob. Solve 2 – Hands-on	1 – Teacher 2 – Prob. Solve
Group B	1 – Prob. Solve 2 – Hands-on	1 – Teacher 2 – Prob. Solve	1 – Technology 2 – Teacher	1 – Hands-on 2 – Technology	1 – Prob. Solve 2 – Hands-on
Group C	1 – Hands-on 2 – Technology	1 – Prob. Solve 2 – Hands-on	1 – Teacher 2 – Prob. Solve	1 – Technology 2 – Teacher	1 – Hands-on 2 – Technology
Group D	1 – Technology 2 – Teacher	1 – Hands-on 2 – Technology	1 – Prob. Solve 2 – Hands-on	1 – Teacher 2 – Prob. Solve	1 – Technology 2 – Teacher

This could also work with larger classes that are divided into five groups. The centers, like I mentioned above, can vary depending on the teacher and class.

Lesson - Work Time - 1 Center
Works for: Short or medium length and any class size

This would be similar to the two center format I described above, however students only travel to one center per day. This is one option if you have short class periods, which I consider 50 minutes or less, and want to incorporate some of the aspects of math workshop every day. Students would have a quick warm-up and mini-lesson on the new concept. This would take 20-30 minutes, depending on the day. The worktime would be about 10 minutes. This would leave you with approximately 10-20 minutes for each group to go to one center and then do any sort of wrap-up or exit slip at the end of class. A possible chart might look like this.

	Monday	Tuesday	Wednesday	Thursday	Friday
Group A	Teacher	Technology	Hands-on	Prob. Solve	Teacher
Group B	Prob. Solve	Teacher	Technology	Hands-on	Prob. Solve
Group C	Hands-on	Prob. Solve	Teacher	Technology	Hands-on
Group D	Technology	Hands-on	Prob. Solve	Teacher	Technology

The downside here, of course, is that students only get to go to one center every day. This means that you will not be able to meet with each student every day in a small group, but rather once per week for most students. Since Group A meets with you twice per week, you may want to consider placing some of your struggling students in Group A, so they can get the extra 10 minutes of teacher support each week!

Regular Lesson - 2 Centers Per Day
Works for: Short length and small class size

One of the factors that can make math workshop difficult to implement is having a short class length. This option is for class lengths of 50 minutes or less and small class sizes. This structure involves a brief warm-up and mini-lesson on the new concept, lasting about 20-30 minutes. Then students would travel to two centers. However, to be sure that all students have a center that is a Homework Center each day, it would be set up something like this.

	Monday	Tuesday	Wednesday	Thursday	Friday
Group A	1 – Homework 2 – Technology	1 – Homework 2 – Hands-on	1 – Homework 2 – Technology	1 – Homework 2 – Hands-on	1 – Homework 2 – Technology
Group B	1 – Homework 2 – Hands-on	1 – Homework 2 – Technology	1 – Homework 2 – Hands-on	1 – Homework 2 – Technology	1 – Homework 2 – Hands-on
Group C	1 – Technology 2 – Homework	1 – Hands-on 2 – Homework	1 – Technology 2 – Homework	1 – Hands-on 2 – Homework	1 – Technology 2 – Homework
Group D	1 – Hands-on 2 – Homework	1 – Technology 2 – Homework	1 – Hands-on 2 – Homework	1 – Technology 2 – Homework	1 – Hands-on 2 – Homework

In this format there is no Teacher Center, which is a drawback. However, depending on your preference, you could substitute a Teacher Center in for either the Hands-on Center or the Technology Center. This would allow you to meet with two groups per day.

These are by no means the only options if you are looking to incorporate math workshop into your daily classroom routine, but rather suggested frameworks to begin thinking about how you can implement math workshop in your classroom, based on your class length and class size. Remember that even if you are only meeting with a small group 2 or 3 times per week, that is still better than not meeting with those students at all! You would be amazed at what you can accomplish and the misconceptions you can clear up with your students by utilizing this small group time.

3 Pros and Cons of Math Workshop

As with all styles of teaching, there are pros and cons that go along with using math workshop in the middle school classroom. How much extra planning will there be? How will it help me differentiate learning with my students? How will it affect behavior management? Thinking through these pros and cons can help you decide if math workshop is something that fits in your classroom.

THE CONS

Behavior Management

Probably the biggest concern that I have heard when it comes to starting math workshop is how it will affect behavior. If the teacher is working with a small group at the front table, how can I ensure that the other students are on task? I remember asking this when I was first considering whether or not I wanted to experiment with math workshop in my classroom. When I asked my school's instructional coach this question, her response has stuck with me to this day. The students that may be off task during math workshop centers are probably going to be the same students that are off task in a traditional setting. It is not necessarily the structure of the class that is causing the behavior, it is how you approach and respond to the behaviors that will make a difference!

I list behavior management as a con, because that is often how it is perceived when it comes to using math workshop. However, I truly believe that the challenges of managing a classroom in a traditional structure are similar to the challenges of managing a classroom in a math workshop structure. Of course, that doesn't mean it's easy! Having solid classroom management may be the most difficult aspect of teaching. When it comes to math workshop, I have found two key factors that help with ensuring that students are on task and doing what they need to be doing! First, setting the expectations for centers early in the year and practicing these expectations. Second is to find ways to hold students accountable for their work at each center. More details about how these can be done are in the following chapters.

Extra Planning and Preparation

Another factor that often comes up when starting math workshop is the amount of planning and preparation that it will require. It is true that math workshop requires more materials, ideas, planning, and preparation. The ideal situation of four centers every day requires teachers to have four different activities planned daily for students. At first, this may seem daunting. However, remember that some of these centers take very little planning once your math workshop is up and running. Once you have task cards or problems printed for your Teacher Center, that center will require almost no preparation. If your district uses a set curriculum, you can likely use homework problems from those resources for the Homework Center. The preparation for this center would be figuring out which problems to assign. Once your Technology Center is set up, this center requires very little planning and preparation. If using Khan Academy, you can easily assign videos and problems through the website. Most other similar programs, such as IXL, can be done individually by students.

The Hands-On Center will probably require the most planning and preparation, but remember, it is perfectly okay to reuse math activities and games! There are a ton of options out there and I encourage you to be creative with the activities and resources that you use during this time. This can be one of your greatest opportunities to make math fun for your students!

Out of Your Comfort Zone

Math workshop is different. I think back to my middle school years, Macarena and all, and only remember being in a traditional math classroom. We had a warm-up, a lesson, and then worked on homework. This structure worked fine for some students, myself included, but looking back I don't think it worked for all students. Math workshop gives all students access to the support of the teacher in a small group. Students who don't learn well in a whole group setting have other opportunities to learn the concepts. However, because it is different than the traditional structure, it can feel uncomfortable at first. Students will be moving around the room, interacting in small groups, and all working on different tasks simultaneously. The more you go out of your comfort zone and experiment with math workshop, the more comfortable you will become with this activity and motion in your classroom.

PROS

Meeting With Every Student in Small Groups

The opportunity to meet with every student in a small group each day makes a huge impact on student learning. It makes it so easy to find out exactly where students are struggling and what you can do to help them. It also provides a great opportunity to question students' thinking and have them explain their mathematical reasoning. In addition to the support you provide students during this small group time, you will also find that students are great at helping each other. I can't count the number of times some of my stronger students finish their task card, see that the student next to them is stuck, and turn to help explain! In addition to the academic benefits of this time, it is also a great opportunity for you to get to know your students. Their quirky, middle school personalities always find their way out during this small group time.

I once had a 6th grade student who I knew was completely obsessed with Star Wars. One day, I decided to make a set of problems for the Teacher Center group that involved the cost of this student and his friends going to the new Star Wars movie. He was so excited to be a part of the Star Wars problem that day that he claimed he would address me as Lord O'Connor for the remainder of the year. I, of course, held him to this, and was greeted with a "Good morning, Lord O'Connor!" every morning for that school year!

I don't think you can overestimate the importance of connecting with every student on a personal level, especially your struggling learners. Math workshop's small group structure gives you daily opportunities to get to know your students and let them know that you believe that they can learn and that you care about them as individuals.

Keeping Students Active

If you have taught middle school students, you know how active and energetic they are. Sitting in the same spot for a whole class period or extended work time is no easy task for an adult, let alone a middle school student. Naturally built in to math workshop are movement breaks. Every ten or fifteen minutes, as students rotate to their next center, they are required to get up and move to a new spot in the classroom. Whether they realize it or not, these movement breaks are an integral part of their learning. The different centers allow you the opportunity to create comfortable spots for students to learn. Do you have a bean bag area? Do you have other comfortable seating options in your classroom? The Hands-on Center is a perfect opportunity to use seating areas such as these.

Differentiation

Math workshop also provides a number of ways to differentiate learning with your students. As you meet with each student in a small group, it is important to have a set of basic problems and a set of enrichment problems. As I described in Chapter 1, I use my Task Cards and Enrichment Task Cards, to serve this purpose. These allow you to meet the needs of your students who are struggling, while also meeting the needs of your higher achieving students by challenging them with enrichment problems. The Technology Center also provides some opportunity to differentiate. Many online programs allow you to assign specific sets of problems to specific students. Although it requires a bit more planning, I have also differentiated homework assignments in the past. I will create two assignments for each day. The first assignment includes more basic problems for that concept. The second assignment includes fewer problems that are at a much higher level. I can then assign these to students or let them pick which assignment they will complete.

Making Math Fun

Making math fun has always been one of my primary goals as a middle school math teacher. Many students come in with a negative perception of math because of frustrations they have had in the past. Embedded in the framework of math workshop are opportunities to make math fun.

Want to incorporate an online math site or game into your class? You can plug this into your Technology Center. Or do you want to create some friendly competition in your classroom? Find a math game to use during your Hands-On Center. The math centers can be flexible, so whatever awesome idea you find from another teacher, you can almost always incorporate it into the math workshop framework as a new math center.

4 Behavior Management

Behavior management can be difficult in any type of classroom. Middle school students are full of energy and enthusiasm. Combining that energy with a desire for students to interact and fit in with their peers makes managing behavior no easy task! When it comes to classroom management during math workshop, you have to find out what works for you and your style of teaching. Having consequences for students who are not following expectations is important and can vary depending on your school. One of my goals has been to prevent these behaviors as much as possible before they happen. I focus on the following two aspects when creating activities.

Hold Students Accountable

It is important to make sure students are held accountable for the work they are doing at centers. This sense of accountability for students will help to keep them on task and learning math at their math centers. When writing about math workshop, Newton writes, "It is really important to have structures in place to hold the children accountable for their work" (2016, p. 98). Figuring out what these structures look like in your classroom, for each of the centers, is important to have set before jumping into math workshop with your students. Holding students accountable can mean different things at each of the different centers.

Typically, at the Teacher Center, there are very few behavior issues. The close proximity to you, as the teacher, and individualized attention each student receives usually prevents any major behaviors at this center. If using a white board table, I do recommend sectioning off a personal space for each student using tape. Before I thought to do that, I occasionally had students that would have their work encroach into another student's space on the table, which can cause unnecessary conflict!

In my experience, the Homework Center also has very few behavior problems arise. Most middle school students are motivated to get their work done in class so they don't have to bring it home. Requiring students to be at their assigned seat during this center can help them focus on their own work. There are times during math workshop to be working in groups and times to be working individually. The homework is each student's opportunity to practice the new concept individually.

During the Technology Center, I have found it fairly simple to hold students accountable. As I stated earlier, I use a combination of Khan Academy and IXL with my classes. Both of these programs make it easy to track student activity and progress from your teacher account. One of my fellow teachers also had the great idea of projecting the Khan Academy activity on the projector during math workshop. Every student was required to have 10 minutes of work complete before they left class. The Top Ten prizes I described in Chapter 1 have also provided extra motivation for my students to stay focused during the Technology Center. Every Friday, the top ten students in each class receive a prize. It is a fun way to end the week, rewarding the students who worked hard during that center for the week. The Top Ten can change categories from week to week. Depending on the site you are using, you can track questions attempted, questions answered correctly, points earned, and much more! The number one student each week gets a pack of gum in my class, while the second and third place get a piece of candy. Number four through ten get the choice of a mint or Starburst!

Behavior management during the Hands-on Center is often the part of math workshop that is most intimidating for teachers. Middle school students working in small groups, on a hands-on activity, without direct teacher supervision... now that is a scary thought, right? Two important things to consider while planning this center can help keep students on task. First, make sure the activities are engaging. If the activity isn't something that students can enjoy doing, it will be difficult to keep them on task. Second, hold students accountable by having them turn something in. If it's a math game, have them turn in their work from the game. If it is another type of math activity, have them take a picture and send you their final product before cleaning up. Holding students accountable to accomplish their task during this time is important, especially with middle school students.

Find Engaging Activities

When planning your hands-on activities for math workshop, spend that extra time finding activities that will make math engaging for your students. A hands-on activity doesn't mean printing and copying a worksheet and having students complete the ten problems. That might be okay for the Homework Center, but the Hands-on Center should be something fun. I have spent hours creating math center activities that can be used at this center in the middle school classroom. The Resources Index at the end of the book gives an overview of some of these activities. I also encourage you to head over to the Teachers Pay Teachers website and find some of the outstanding middle school teacher-authors out there. There are a plethora of free and paid resources available for the middle school math classroom!

What to Do When Students Are Off Task

Before starting math workshop, it is only natural to wonder how students will respond to new classroom routines and what will happen when students aren't following expectations. As I stated earlier, when I was first starting math workshop, one of my colleagues made a point that hit home and helped ease some of my concerns about how students would behave during math workshop centers. She made the comment that the students who I would have behavior difficulties with during math workshop would also be students who I was having behavior difficulties with in the traditional setting. Regardless of the classroom structure, it was important to find ways to get these students back on track and headed in the right direction. However you handle and manage your behavior now can be easily adapted to a math workshop setting. The important part is to have a system that students know and follow through with consequences. One example would be to first give students a verbal warning if they are off task at a center. The second time you ask, students must go back to their seat and work on that activity individually. If that still is not effective, you may need to keep the student after class, contact parents, etc. Of course, this is not the only system. The most important thing is to have a system that works for you and your students and stick with it.

Planning for Substitute Teachers

As you have now gathered, math workshop is full of routines  and expectations for students. In my experience, I have found it difficult for substitute teachers to be thrown into a classroom that is using math workshop. I would often come back to find something like this! If you teach middle school, I bet you have seen this before! After subbing for a year out of college, I understand how challenging it can be to jump into a class that is not yours and attempt to keep things as "normal" as possible for the students. When a substitute is needed, I typically plan a more traditional class structure to make life a little bit easier.

5 Getting Math Workshop Started

Changing the way your classroom operates can be intimidating. As teachers, we love routines, and any change from your "normal" classroom structure will feel odd at first. If you decide to begin implementing math workshop in your classroom, stick with it! During the first few days and weeks there will be an adjustment for you and for your students as routines are learned, expectations are set, and math workshop becomes the new "normal" in your classroom. This chapter lays out some key points to keep in mind while getting things started.

The First Few Weeks

Much like the first few weeks of the school year are different than the remainder of the year, the initial few weeks of math workshop will be different. Students will be learning routines, figuring out where they are supposed to be, and adapting to the new structure. Remaining consistent with your routines and expectations from day one of math workshop is critical. As Newton states, "Children work well when they know what to expect, when there are rules, rewards, and consequences, and when these are immediate and consistent from the beginning of the school year" (2016, p. 40). Ideally, you will be starting math workshop at the beginning of a new school year. This is the best case scenario, since there are no routines already in place that need to be changed. Math workshop will become your classroom routine!

With that being said, it is completely possible to begin implementing math workshop in the middle of the school year. When I first began, I started my math centers coming back from our winter break. You would be surprised at how easily students adapt to a new structure. After a few weeks, they will have forgotten they ever did it differently!

I have found it helps to have a very simple lesson for the first few days you are implementing math workshop. Make it a review lesson that the majority of your students already understand and can feel confident doing. This will allow you and your students to focus on learning the routines of math workshop and prevent students from getting frustrated with the content. Students will be nervous about figuring out what center they travel to, who is in their group, and what they are supposed to be doing. If they become too frustrated with the content during these early days, they won't be able to learn the routines of math workshop and could have a negative perception of math in the future!

Creating Your Groups

When thinking about which students fit where, remember that other than the group that travels to the Homework Center first, it really does not matter what group students are a part of. If you are running the full math workshop model where students are traveling to every center every day, they will all get to each center at some point during the class. It is very important that the group that begins at the

Homework Center is made up of students who can handle starting on the homework without meeting with you at the Teacher Center first.

Creating your groups at the start of the year can be somewhat of a challenge. If it is early in the school year, you may not have a good feel for which students work well together and which students do not. You also may not know which students will be able to handle beginning at the Homework Center. It might be worth contacting their teacher from last year to help pinpoint a few of the stronger math students that could fit in this group!

Planning and Preparation

Planning is an integral part of math workshop, especially during the first few weeks. Having a week or two planned out will help you get off to a good start. The first week will be focused on routines and expectations, so finding resources and games that are fairly simple for students to complete is helpful. You want students to leave that first week feeling confident and successful in the math classroom!

Along with math workshop comes some additional preparation. Prior to each week, I recommend going through each day of your lesson plans and thinking about what materials you will need to prepare. I spent some time in the summer printing, copying, and laminating all of the regular task cards and enrichment task cards that I use throughout the school year. You should only need about 6-7 copies of each task card, since that would most likely be the size of your largest group. Having these task cards copied and prepared for the entire year was a huge time saver once the school year started.

The Hands-on Center is the other center that will probably require some preparation each week. Whatever games and activities you have planned for that week, it helps to have them prepped and ready to go prior to the week. With math workshop, the laminator will become your best friend! I don't know how many times I have made copies and prepped a math game, didn't laminate it, and ended up having to reprint it the following year. It's definitely worth the extra time to have all of these materials laminated and ready to use again!

If you haven't already asked yourself the question "How do I organize and store all of these materials?" you will at some point. This is such a difficult task that I devoted all of the next chapter to organizing your math workshop materials!

Practice Routines

The goal of the first day, and even the first few weeks, is for students to become comfortable with the routines and transitions of math workshop. The first few days, instead of working with the Teacher Center group, it may help to walk around the room as students are working in their centers, monitoring and assisting as needed. You can give the Teacher Center group some simple task cards or problems to work on during that time.

Before starting, make sure you know where you want each group to be located. In my room, I work with the Teacher Center group at my front rectangular white board table. The Homework Center and the Technology Center students work individually at their seats. I require these students to be at their assigned seat to help with focus and productivity during these two centers. Students at the Hands-on Center can work in one of the corners of my room. I have pillows and small tables in one corner, bean bags and small tables in another corner, and a second white board table in my back corner. Below is a diagram that depicts my classroom setup. Of course, everyone's classroom might look different based on size, shape, number of students, and available furniture.

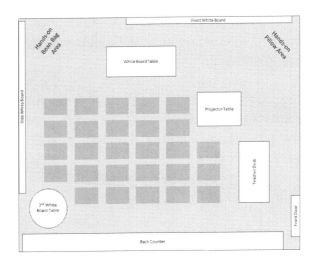

Make the focus of that first week getting students comfortable with the routines of math workshop. Be very clear with what should be happening at each center, the noise level that is expected, and how students should be transitioning from one center to another. Students may be confused about which center they should be at the first day or two. Having a poster, similar to the one shown, can help students keep track of where they should be working at any given time!

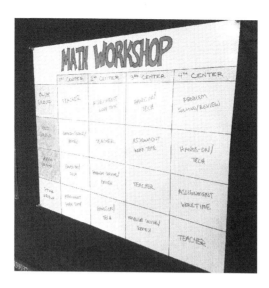

Setting Expectations

Setting expectations and practicing how students should be acting during math workshop is a key factor in determining how successful it will be. The first weeks should be focused more on these expectations and routines than academic concepts. Our first unit of math includes mostly review concepts, which fits nicely with setting up the routines and expectations of math workshop. If this isn't the case for you, it might be worth adding in some days of review to begin the school year!

My first expectation addresses students focus during math workshop. It is extremely important that students stay focused on the task at hand and understand that there are consequences if they aren't doing what is expected. Come in to the first day with a plan for what will happen if a student is at one of the centers and not on task. I also think it is important to discuss this with students prior to starting the first day of math workshop, so that they know what will happen if they lose focus and it isn't a surprise to them! I have a set of consequences where they get one verbal reminder. After the first verbal reminder, if they need another they go back to their seat. If a third reminder is needed, I meet with them after class and will sometimes call home.

Another expectation to be clear about is the noise level. With so much going on at the same time, math workshop can naturally get a little bit noisier than a traditional classroom. A noisy classroom can simply mean students are engaged and learning, however it is important for students to understand what noise level they are using. Whatever system you or your school uses, be sure students know what noise level is expected at each center. Our school uses a numbered noise level system from 0 to 4, as indicated.

0 – Silent
1 – Whisper
2 – Classroom Voice
3 – Outside Voice
4 – Emergency Voice

I expect the Teacher Center to be at a level 2 or less. Students are mostly working on their own at this center, but may be interacting with the teacher or the other group members as they work through the task card problems. I expect the Homework Center and Technology Center to be a level 0. These are independent work times for the students. The only exception would be if they need to quietly ask a question to one of their peers about the homework. The Hands-on Center should be a level 2 or less, depending on the activity. It can be easy for students at the Hands-on Center to forget about their volume and get a little bit too loud as they get excited about whatever game or activity they are working on. It is important to remind them early on of the noise level expectations.

Also be clear about your expectations when it is time to rotate and where in the room each student should be during their centers. Once my students have practiced the routine of transitioning, I can simply say "It is time to quickly and quietly rotate to your next center" and students can transition in about 30-45 seconds. The first few days or weeks, I physically have everybody pause and discuss how we are going to transition, stressing that it should be quiet, materials should be cleaned up from their previous center, and students should move quickly to their next center. The first few days, you will also probably want to actually tell each group where they are going. It is not uncommon to have a few confused students or groups as they transition those first few days! Once transitioned, students should have a clear expectation of where in the room they should be working. This is completely up to you to decide and depends a lot on the layout of your classroom. My Teacher Center is at the front table, Homework Center is at their seats, Technology Center is at their seats, and the Hands-On Center is located in the two front corners of my room. These corners have bean bags and pillows for students to use as they work on the floor.

A final expectation that I have during math workshop is also one of the most important expectations. While I am working with students at the front table during the Teacher

Center, students should not interrupt me to ask questions. Your time at the Teacher Center should be completely devoted to the group at the front table. This is the most important time of math workshop and also the time where you can make the biggest impact on students, whether they are struggling with a concept or in need of an extra challenge to stretch their thinking! Even if a student is stuck on a homework problem, they should find a different solution to help them work through it. Some options may be to ask another adult in the room, quietly ask another student, or skip it and come back to it later. If they are really stuck on a problem, I will often recommend for them to skip it and come see me quickly at the end of class. The only exception I have for coming to me at the front table is if they have a pass filled out for the bathroom or locker for me to sign. This is something I can do quickly, without interrupting my work with the group at the front table. This expectation can be difficult for students for the first few weeks of running math workshop. However, I have found that if you are consistent with telling students that they should not interrupt the Teacher Center for these initial weeks, they learn quickly that they need to find another solution!

Setting these expectations, and any others that you feel you need to add, is a vital part of running a successful math workshop. If students are not able to work independently at their centers, you won't be able to devote the attention and assistance needed to the students at the Teacher Center. To help reiterate these expectations, consider making some sort of poster that gives students a visual of the expectations.

6 Keeping Your Materials Organized

One of the biggest challenges that comes with math workshop is finding an effective way to organize your math workshop materials. The longer you teach, the more math games, activities, and resources you will accumulate. That means finding a way to organize and store these materials is essential. After an exhausting day of teaching, spending the extra minute to put things back where they belong can save you fifteen minutes the next time you need it! Every teacher's situation, classroom space, and materials are different, so there is never going to be a one size fits all organizational solution. In this chapter, I will lay out what I have found to work in my classroom, given the resources that I use and the space that I have. I have gotten to this point of organization through trial and error, trying something new every year until it works. Hopefully, you can pick and choose ideas from this chapter to help you organize your math workshop resources.

Task Cards

It took me a long time to learn to keep my task cards organized. I fell into the terrible habit of using the task cards needed for a lesson and then just setting them in a pile on my desk or a table. That pile gradually grew into a mountain of unorganized task card chaos! I would then spend hours at the end of the semester or school year reorganizing all of these task cards by topic.

The solution I came up with were these bins from Michaels craft store. They ended up being a perfect size to store my math workshop task cards. Each of my cards is approximately the size of one half of a piece of paper. With six copies of each task card printed and laminated, I can fit an entire year of my 6th grade regular task cards into two of these bins, organized by unit. My 6th grade enrichment task cards are also in two bins, also organized by unit. As I started teaching my 8th grade math class, five years into my teaching career, I organized those task cards in the same way. Using cardstock, I created dividers to place in between each unit of task cards.

This method has worked unbelievably well, as long as you take the time to put the task cards back each day after using them! Just take the front set of task cards from the bin and when you return them, put them at the back of the bin. That way, you will always have that day's task cards ready to go and waiting at the front of your task card bins!

Math Games and Activities

As you start incorporating math games and other hands-on activities into your daily routine, you will start to accumulate a ridiculous amount of cards and boards. In my opinion, these have been the toughest math workshop materials to organize. I was consistently trying a new method of organization every year. Finally, I found a system that worked well enough to stay organized for an entire school year.

In my room I have two file cabinets that were left by the retired teacher who preceded me. In these cabinets, I store all of the game boards and resources that are the size of a regular piece of computer paper. This includes my bingo boards, math board game boards, scavenger hunts, and more. I use sticky notes to separate and organize these boards.

 Since many of these games also have smaller pieces, I then needed a place to store the myriad of playing cards, math sort cards, and other small game pieces that went along with the games. I ordered these

stackable bins through my school order from Office Depot. Using cardstock, I labeled each bin by sliding a small piece of cardstock into the front slot of the bin and labeling with the type of activity. As you can see, I have a bin for many of the different types of games and resources that I use throughout the school year. These bins are stored on a bookshelf that is directly behind my desk, making it easy to access on a daily basis.

Organizing Weekly Materials

I personally like to be organized for an entire week in advance... or at least that is the goal. Below the stackable bins on my bookshelf, I set aside two shelves that have spots labeled Monday through Friday. Every week before I leave school on Friday, I lay out the materials needed for each day the following week. Math games, math sorts, worksheets, and whatever else I need for that week are copied and placed on the day that they will be used.

Trying to stay consistent with this helps me be prepared for the upcoming week. I can come in Monday morning knowing that I have all of the materials ready to go and waiting. I won't be caught off guard having to make last minute copies of a game or activity. Of course, this is easier said than done and like every teacher, there are plenty of weeks where I am getting resources cut and prepped on the fly!

Posting Homework Assignments

Having a consistent location where homework is posted can also help cut down on the number of unnecessary questions from students about the homework assignment. In my room, I have an assignment notebook board. Each day has a 1 and a 2, which refers to what we are doing in class that day and the page of the homework assignment, respectively. I post the exact problem numbers of the homework assignment next to this assignment board.

I have also found I save a lot of time by posting the entire list of homework assignments for a unit on my window next to this board. This can save you a ton of time when you have absent students who are coming in to get the homework assignment that they missed. If you have it posted, you can just refer them to the homework list! At first I was hesitant to post future assignments, fearing that students may work ahead. However, I have really had no issues with this happening and even if it did happen, I think it would only benefit students to be looking ahead at what we are learning in the coming days.

When it comes to getting students to turn in homework on time, one routine I started to incorporate was our classroom homework data. Each day, I began calculating the percentage of students in each class that had their homework turned in on time. I calculated this separately for each class and then graphed these trends over time. It was fun to see students get excited about trying to beat other classes or trying to reach 100% as a class! This was by no means a miracle cure to get every student turning in homework, however it did help put a little pressure on students to get their work done, without singling them out and embarrassing them in front of the class. It was also a fun way to incorporate graphing into an everyday classroom routine!

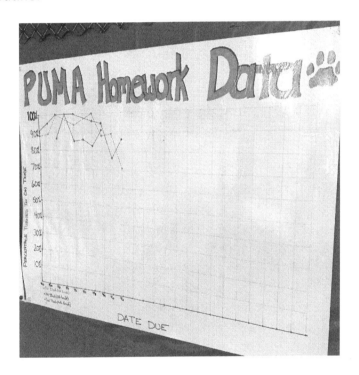

7 White Board Table

If there is one classroom tool I cannot live without, it is my front white board table! When I first began using math workshop in my classroom, my students had been using some old white boards during our Teacher Center. They would bring one of these white boards with them to the Teacher Center and complete the task card problems on their personal board. Although using these personal white boards worked, it presented a few problems. Towards the end of the year, these boards started to peel, break, and turn every color BUT white. It also added the additional wasted time of students needing to get their white board. Additionally, students often tilted the boards towards themselves as they worked, making it difficult for me to monitor their work! I wanted to find a way to eliminate these problems from my routine and make my class run more efficiently.

Creating the White Board Table

This is about the time I started to think about creating a white board table to use as my front table. This chapter focuses on the creation and longevity of this white board table. Here is the table I started with. It was a very dark brown and had a very smooth surface.

My first step, was to prime the table. My table was such a dark brown to begin with, I thought this was necessary. I wanted to make sure that if I was going to try this project that it turned out, so I decided to take the extra step of priming it. If the table was white or a lighter color to begin with, then I would have considered skipping the primer. I didn't end up sanding the table at all, although that might not be a bad idea. I actually didn't think of it until it was too late! I used a bunch of tape to line the side of the table so that it wouldn't get any primer or paint on it. I used a few coats of the KILZ 2 Latex Primer.

After getting the primer on, I went home and gave it about 24 hours to dry. When I came back, I got out the dry-erase paint kit I had purchased. For about $20, I bought the Rust-Oleum Dry Erase Paint. I was a little skeptical going in, since this was the "cheap" option and I had read some not so great reviews of the paint. I followed the directions on the box, giving the table two coats of the dry erase paint. I used a foam roller that was designed to paint smooth surfaces. Once you mix the paint together, you only have an hour to use the paint. I did one coat, let it dry for about 25 minutes, and then added the second coat. It was as easy as that! The toughest part was waiting the three days before trying it out!

Now that my table is in use, I make sure that I test out all of my markers on a different white board before using it on the table. For some reason, my green Expo markers always have a tough time erasing, so I am making sure I don't use those. My sixth grade students are always beyond excited when I first show them the table at the start of the year!

Durability of the Table

As I went through my first year of using the white board table and started posting pictures on social media, one of the most common questions that I received was about the durability of the table. How was it holding up? Was it staying that clean white color? Remember, I used the cheaper paint, which made me a little nervous about how the table would hold up!

On a scale of 1-10, I would give the table about a 7.5 when it comes to durability. This is after pretty heavy use by my middle school students. Each spot on the table gets used by twelve groups per day, which means twelve students per spot. Each student is doing approximately five problems each day at that spot. That adds up to each spot being used and erased about sixty times per day! Here is what the table looked like after about three months of heavy use.

It's a little tough to see with the glare, but the heavily used spots are definitely not perfectly white. This doesn't really bother me. For how much students enjoy using it and how convenient it is to use during math workshop, it is definitely worth it. Other than it not being perfectly shiny, the only other minor issue has been a few small chips or cracks in the paint. The past few years, I have been repainting the table each summer before the new school year begins. This gives each group of students a nice, shiny, white board table to start the school year with!

An End of Year Tradition

As I began repainting the table for each school year, I decided to make a tradition of signing the white board table. At the end of each year, all of my students get to come up and sign the white board table in Sharpie! This end of year tradition has been a huge hit and is fun for students. The idea of using a Sharpie on the white board table always creates a funny reaction from my students!

8 Resources Index

Beginning math workshop can be intimidating from a planning and resources point of view. Having four separate centers in which students participate each day requires planning and prepping four separate activities. With that being said, it is important to keep in mind a couple of things. First, it is perfectly okay to have a center be the same game or activity on multiple days. At first it might seem as though students would get bored having the center be the same, but remember that each center is only 10-15 minutes of each student's day. Second, don't feel like you need to create every new activity that you use. If creating them is something you enjoy, then go for it! If not, there are plenty of free and paid resources and ideas out there! This index highlights a few of my most useful and engaging resources that I have either created or found, organized by the center where I use them.

Daily Check Resources

As mentioned in Chapter 1, the following exit slip questions are used as my "Daily Check" at the beginning of each class period. Each topic includes four questions that increase in difficulty, from beginning to advanced. These serve as a perfect daily check in to see how your students are doing with each concept.

TpT Store: Middle School Math Man

6th Grade Math Exit Slips Full Year Bundle
8th Grade Math Exit Slips Full Year Bundle

Teacher Center Resources

At the Teacher Center, task cards are my go to resource. For each group that comes to the front table, I have a set of regular task cards and a set of enrichment task cards. Having taught both 6th and 8th grade, I have full year sets available for each grade in my Teachers Pay Teachers store. Following are the sets of task cards that I use for the entire school year. Within each of these bundles there is a free unit of task cards that you can try out to see if they are the correct level for your students!

TpT Store: Middle School Math Man

Math Task Cards Full-Year Bundle – 6th Grade Math

Math Enrichment Full-Year Bundle – 6th Grade Math Task Cards

8th Grade Math Task Cards Full Year Bundle

8th Grade Math Enrichment Task Cards Full Year Bundle

Technology Center Resources

For my Technology Center, I have primarily used either the Khan Academy website or IXL program. I highly recommend both! Listed below are the two websites if you would like more information.

www.khanacademy.org

www.ixl.com/math/

Hands-On Center Resources

There are so many opportunities to find engaging resources for you students at the Hands-On Center. I have found a passion in creating engaging resources that my students can use during math class. Following are a few of my favorites! I hope you find some of these useful as well!

TpT Store: Middle School Math Man

Math board games have become a huge hit in my classroom. Students enjoy the competition of a game and they are a great way to make practicing math skills more exciting! Following are some of the different bundles of math board games that are available in my TpT store.

Fractions and Decimals Board Game Bundle

Expressions, Equations, and Inequalities Board Game Bundle

Area and Volume Board Game Bundle

Statistics and Probability Board Game Bundle

Another one of my students' favorites are math sorts. In these sorts, students must sort the cards based on their answers. Once sorted, they flip over the cards and unscramble the funny phrases on the back!

6th Grade Math Sort Bundle

8th Grade Math Sort Bundle

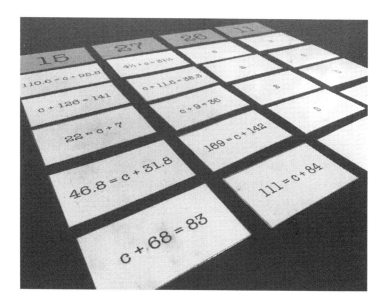

Math bingo games can be a fun whole group or small group center activity. I have three bingo games available individually or as a part of the following bundle. The bundle includes Multiplication Bingo, Negative Number Bingo, and Squares and Roots Bingo.

Math Bingo Bundle

I have plenty of other resources available in my store that I would encourage you to check out if you are interested in stocking up on math workshop resources! For a full year's worth of materials, be sure to check out my two Mega Bundles listed below

Math Workshop Full Year Mega Bundle (For Upper Elementary/Middle School Math)

Math Mega Bundle (8th Grade Math)

Other Useful Resources

Here are a few of the other sites I would highly recommend checking out if you have not already.

Inside Mathematics Website

I love the www.insidemathematics.org website. Specifically, I have often used their free Problems of the Month. Each of these include an overarching problem that gets progressively more challenging for students. It is a great option for students that are working at their own pace or to use as group work problems.

Illustrative Mathematics

The Illustrative Mathematics website at www.illustrativemathematics.org also has some amazing math resources.

References

Hoffer, A. (2012). Minds on Mathematics: Using Math Workshop to Develop Deep Understanding in Grades 4-8. Portsmouth, NH: Heinemann.

Newton, N. (2016). Math Workshop in Action: Strategies for Grades K-5. New York, NY: Routledge.

About the Author

Alex O'Connor is a public school teacher and education blogger from Wisconsin. He has spent much of his teaching career in the 6th and 8th grade math classroom.

Alex O'Connor lives with his wife, Nicole, and son, Finn, in a small town in Wisconsin. He is an avid baseball fan, player, and high school coach.

You can follow along with the "Middle School Math Man" in the following ways.

Follow on Facebook
www.facebook.com/middleschoolmathman

Follow on Instagram
@middleschoolmathman

Made in the USA
Lexington, KY
15 June 2019